Wild One

Also by Lucille Lang Day

Fire in the Garden
Self-Portrait with Hand Microscope

Wild One

Poems by

Lucille Lang Day

Scarlet Tanager
BOOKS

Cover photograph: Lucille Lang Day, age 16, with daughter Liana, nine months, in 1964.

Back cover photograph by George Paul Csicsery.

Design: DuFlon Design, Berkeley, CA
Composition: Archetype Typography, Berkeley, CA

Published by Scarlet Tanager Books
P.O. Box 20906
Oakland, CA 94620

Publisher's Cataloging-in-Publication
(Provided by Quality Books, Inc.)

Day, Lucille.
　　Wild one : poems / by Lucille Lang Day. --
　1st ed.
　　　p. cm.
　　　LCCN: 00-130149
　　　ISBN: 0-9670224-3-6

　　　1. Women--Poetry.　2. Mothers and daughters--
　Poetry.　I. Title.

PS3554.A965W55 2000　　　　　811'.6
　　　　QBI00-131

Acknowledgments

I am indebted to poets Marcia Falk, Alicia Suskin Ostriker, and Steven Rood for invaluable critical feedback on these poems. I also wish to thank the editors of the following publications, in which some of the poems have appeared:

Alkali Flats: "MRI Scan"

Anthology of Magazine Verse & Yearbook of American Poetry (Monitor Book Company): "Reject Jell-O"

Berkeley Poetry Review: "First Wedding"

Berkeley Poets' Cooperative: "Night Lights Over Jackass Hill," "Patterns," "Poem to Give to a Lover," "Winter Nap," "Woman in Blue Jeans and Wool Socks"

Berkeley Poets' Cooperative Anthology (Berkeley Poets' Workshop and Press): "Patterns"

Blue Unicorn: "After the Earthquake," "Fall," "The Gambler's Daughter," "Phone Call," "Poem for My Daughters," "Pretty Poems," "Shoplifter"

The Book of Birth Poetry (Virago Press, Great Britain; Bantam Books, USA): "The Abortion," "Labor"

California Quarterly: "Fifth Birthday," "Jeff," "Slip and Slide"

The Chattahoochee Review: "Birth Mothers," "Snapshot"

Epos: "The Lab"

The Hawaii Pacific Review: "A Friendship"

The Hudson Review: "Applying for AFDC," "Bomb Threat," "Christmas Eve at the Cemetery," "Fifteen," "King of the Mountain," "Neurochemist," "Red Shoes," "Reject Jell-O"

It's All the Rage! Poems About Suicide and Its Alternatives (Andrew Mountain Press): "Why I'm Not Going to Commit Suicide"

Lookings & Listenings (Alameda Poets): "The Abortion," "Amelia Davis"

The Lucid Stone: "In Paradise with My Daughter"

Maryland Poetry Review: "Converting"

A More Perfect Union: Poems and Stories About the Modern Wedding (St. Martin's): "Reject Jell-O"

Mother Songs (W.W. Norton): "Fifteen"

New CollAge Magazine: "The Resumé, 1994"

Panoply: "Meeting Again"

Pinyon Poetry: "November Collage"

Poet Lore: "Here We Are in Blackhawk," "The Owl"

Poetry Tonight (www.poetrytonight.com): "Driving Home"

Poets & Peace International: "Intensive Care"

Portland Review: "Middle Age," "Something Right"

Pudding Magazine: "Scenes from a Divorce," "Vanity"

River Oak Review: "Biology Student"

Rooms: "Response"

Slant: "Wine and Roses"

The Threepenny Review: "The Qualifying Exam"

US1 Worksheets: "Labor," "Looking Back"

Voices International: "The Picnic"

Voices Within the Ark: The Modern Jewish Poets: (Avon Books): "Labor"

The Walrus: "1954"

The Wolf Head Quarterly: "Birdman in the Basement"

Writing For Our Lives: "Anorexia," "The Hot Tub"

"Converting" received Third Prize in the 1998 Barbara T. Ewing Poetry Contest of the *Maryland Poetry Review.*

The following poems appeared in a limited-edition chapbook, *Self-Portrait with Hand Microscope* (Berkeley Poets' Workshop and Press): "The Abortion," "Amelia Davis," "Applying for AFDC," "Fifteen," "First Wedding," "The Gambler's Daughter," "I Wanted a Baby," "The Lab," "Labor," "Nature Poems," "Neurochemist," "Patterns," "Poem to Give to a Lover," "Reject Jell-O," "Woman in Blue Jeans and Wool Socks."

For my father, Richard Allen Lang,
and in memory of my mother, Evelyn Hazard Lang

Contents

Wild One

1954

I danced on the slanted cellar roof
to make it rattle, and when Uncle Dick
yelled, "Stop!" I climbed the fence and ran
toward the creek, cutting through backyards
and hiding between houses. "Geronimo!"
he called, following with long strides,
"Come back!" I slid down the bank, grabbing
at twigs and horsetails, and crossed quickly,
balancing on stones. One foot on the trunk
of my favorite oak, I pulled myself up
into scaly branches, as Uncle Dick,
hands on hips, approached the creek.
"That child's a wild one," he said,
shaking his head. I bit my lip
to hold back laughter, my breath soft
as the wingbeats of insects that skirred
the near leaves. Slender, luminous
blue bodies darted from my palm,
impossible to catch, and disappeared.

Snapshot

There aren't very many photos of my father, Uncle Dick
and me, because we were the ones who took
the pictures, but I have one snapped after dessert
in a neighbor's dining room, when I was twelve or thirteen
and had already started to go bad—a hell-bent gamine.

Fat Cousin Jan and our mothers, the twins, sit
at the table. The photo is black and white,
but I know my sweater is lavender, my skirt purple.
The table is cluttered with cups and dishes; the cloth is lace.
Someone's head is obscured by Jan's moonlike face.

My dad, Uncle Dick and I stand behind the table.
Like me, Jan would soon be incorrigible.
Uncle Dick adored her. She was his dumpling,
but he hit her with a yardstick to make her eat.
She weighed a hundred fifty pounds when she was eight.

I can't remember the purpose of this gathering.
Perhaps there was none. My happy-go-lucky dad is smiling.
He had a secret life: gambling was his passion.
Mom and Aunt Edna had each recovered
from a nervous breakdown, but they still bickered

over who said what, whose daughter was the Queen
of Sheba. I grew up with thorns in my brain,
but my dad was oblivious. He didn't seem to hear them
nagging Jan and me or going berserk
over which of us got the bigger flower on her slice of cake.

I suppose he was ruthless in the card room,
but he didn't drink hard or molest me. I'd give him
a valentine any day. I ran with the rough kids,
drank beer in the hills with my boyfriends, and often cut
school, driven by something—angel or demon—I had to create.

The Gambler's Daughter

Before I knew my ABCs I learned to deal.
I performed at Daddy's Friday night
poker parties. I got to stay up late,
a good thing: I was afraid of the dark.
Sometimes, alone in my room, I saw the nights
as a deck of cards, stacked against me.

On Sundays Daddy and I fed the ducks
at Lake Merritt. Mallards scrambled for crumbs.
Swans drifted past the caged bald eagle.
Canada geese everywhere. Their calls
mingled with the bells from Our Lady of Lourdes,
and coots swam in pools of orange light.

I learned to read the handicaps when I was six.
I picked Lover's Dream and Lucky Lucy,
and Daddy took my bets downtown to the bookie
with his and Mama's. Mama and I sat
on her bed, beside the radio, fingers crossed.
She gave me fifty cents whenever she won.

At Steinhart Aquarium Daddy and I saw
batfish, flat, shaped like fans with yellow
tails and fins. Their eyes, black-banded,
twitched while they swam, mouths small pink slits,
opening and closing as they came toward me,
my hand in Daddy's, my nose pressed to the glass.

I looked into their eyes, liking them
better than the rockfish or eels, better
even than Ulysses, the bug-eyed bass.
They seemed to have a message for me
that I couldn't decode. I watched, wondering
if they knew what I knew: they were trapped.

I got my first jackpot when I was seven,
at the Cal-Neva Club just before breakfast.
Daddy shooed me back to the table. I could
hardly swallow my pancakes. He came back
with a red plastic cup filled with nickels
and a stack of keno tickets for me to mark.

I pretended I was the only daughter
of the Brownings or Curies, though there were no
books of poetry or science in our house.
Mama read *TV Guide*, *Modern Screen*
and *True Confessions;* Daddy read *Playboy*,
murder mysteries and science fiction.

I was never very popular with the kids
at school, though I taught them how to play
spit in the ocean, California poker,
lowball and five-card stud. I kept an extra ace
up my sleeve, but I rarely used it. I learned
to take chances; I knew how to bluff.

Anorexia

Flat-chested, ribs protruding,
I always felt fat: bottom-heavy.
Oh, those massive, rippling thighs
spreading whitely as bread dough
on the car seat! At twelve
I thought I'd die if my waist
exceeded twenty-one inches.

My mother always said, "Eat!
Your bones are showing."
And in the newspaper there was a man,
both legs amputated, fat gnawed
by rats, down to the bone.
My rats were on the inside,
eating outward, consuming my breasts,
drinking the blood from my womb.

I wanted to be beautiful, but
my muscles twitched involuntarily
as I measured and counted every
bite of food. In my dreams
conveyor belts rolled by, loaded
with French fries, hot fudge sundaes,
cheeseburgers, doughnuts, steak.
I grabbed with bare hands
and pressed the food to my face
before waking, trembling with guilt—
ilium, clavicle, carpus, rib exposed.

Shoplifter

I specialized in Elvis Presley records,
makeup, cheap jewelry and angora sweaters.
I did it for the risk and pleasure.
On my way home, I'd stop at the gas station
at the corner of Grand and Linda to scrawl
"Eileen is a whore" on the restroom mirror.

I was caught twice: once at Payless,
where a lady detective with a penguin's build
saw my cousin, age ten, take a bottle
of nail polish—Barn Red. I should have run.
The kid pointed at my bulging black purse
and said, "*She* took more. Look in *there*."

The other time was at Safeway with Eileen,
my best friend. We were caught taking cat food,
mayonnaise and bread. The manager grabbed
the bag from Eileen's hand as we tried to leave
the store. "What an awful lunch!" he said.
"For a better sandwich, I recommend tuna."

So Fine

I was thirteen, feeling high,
when we walked by the Mosswood Motel
and stopped to kiss at Van's
gas station on the corner.

Jim held a bottle of Gallo burgundy
in a brown bag in one hand.
With the other he stroked my rear,
saying, "You are *so* fine."

I thought of his wife, back
at the house. Still, I drank the wine
from his mouth. A cat
with a bird in its teeth appeared.

Being bad, I closed my eyes
and ran my fingers
through Jim's hair. I felt alive, unlike
that bird, a woman to be feared.

I Wanted a Baby

More than anything that Christmas Eve
in my room, sunlight easing through the windows,
my parents out at a party, I wanted a baby
with Bill, who didn't complain
when I kept getting up to check the blood.

Black sheath crumpled around my waist,
eyes shut, I tried to concentrate on names:
Aaron, Eric, Priscilla, Adela.
Bill pressed his lean body against mine
and whispered, "Are you sure it's safe?"

Every day, I woke up hoping to be sick
and dressed in baggy clothes for practice.
My mother marveled at my glow.
Beneath my bed my eighth grade texts rested,
scorned as the stones in my yard.

Now, amazed by muted reds and grays,
limestone and clay in bands that remember
the sea, I remember how people smiled
at me in particular, a real person
at last, with my imaginary child.

First Wedding

If the sky that day had opened not its blue room,
but its gray one, and we had been wed
rain-drenched in Reno, thunder cracking,
it wouldn't have mattered. But the sun was out
to brighten the walls of the old stone church.

All the dolls were long dead by then,
cold and waxy in their cribs and shoe box beds
on closet shelves, dust collecting like memories.
I was fourteen, wearing new white shoes
and my blue-flowered satin Chinese dress.

Mark was three years older, looking skinny
in his rented suit. Our mothers asked the organist
to play "I Love You Truly," and they crooned
and wept. I pretended it was "Love Me Tender."
The men were silent. My father bowed his head.

Standing at the altar, I remembered my blue room.
For years the walls had been shrinking.
I saw myself grown huge like Alice
in a box, small and blue, the door shrunken
to shoe box size. I had to burn my way out.

Now, in the cool light of the sanctuary
all my wounds were soothed. Mark was smiling.
It was hard not to giggle, saying "I do,"
and when we knelt I thought my dress would rip,
but it held, and my hand grew heavy with diamonds.

Afterward we went outside for pictures
to put in our white and gold vinyl book.
We stood under leaves, before a wall of stone,
and now I stare at the girl in the blue Chinese dress.
O child behind my mirror, smiling, trapped.

Fifteen

I was pregnant that year,
stitching lace and purple-flowered ribbon
to tiny kimonos and sacques.
I still thought sperm
came out like pollen dust in puffs of air.

I ate cream of wheat for breakfast, unsalted,
diapered a rubber doll
in my Red Cross baby care class, and sold
lipsticks and gummy lotions to housewives
to pay for a crib.

Oh, it was something, giving birth.
When my water bag splattered
I screamed, and the neat green anaesthesiologist
said, "Why don't you shut up?"
"Fuck you!" I shrieked.

"Breathe deep," was the last thing
I heard him say.
Ten minutes later I woke up.
The obstetrician with his needle and thread,
busy as a seamstress,

winked at the pink-haired nurse
who brought me my baby girl,
wrinkled and howling.
"She's lovely. I'd like a cheeseburger
and milkshake now," I said.

Summer of '64

At sixteen I rode piggyback on the buddy seat,
a sissy bar rising behind me,
chrome scoop and oil bag gleaming.

I kept my feet up, away
from the pipes, but once, climbing off,
I burned my calf. When Bob

pulled wheelies on Broadway,
I braced myself, and butterfly handlebars
rose high above our heads.

I remember the easy feeling
of slow dancing to "Sweet Dreams" in smoky
biker and cowboy bars,

my head nestled on his shoulder,
my imitation leopard skin boots rubbing
against his heavy black ones.

Night and day we rode; wind
whipped my hair. It was enough
to drink beer, hop on the Harley, wrap

my arms around him and ride
to nowhere in particular,
dust slapping my face as we raced

through the cold, the future hidden
like a secret place
in the woods beyond the road.

Reject Jell-O

The man I married twice—
at fourteen in Reno, again in Oakland
the month before I turned eighteen—
had a night maintenance job at General Foods.
He mopped the tiled floors and scrubbed
the wheels and teeth of the Jell-O machines.
I see him bending in green light,
a rag in one hand,
a pail of foamy solution at his feet.
He would come home at seven a.m.
with a box of damaged Jell-O packages,
including the day's first run,
routinely rejected, and go to sleep.
I made salad with that reject Jell-O—
lemon, lime, strawberry, orange, peach—
in a kitchen where I could almost touch
opposing walls at the same time
and kept a pie pan under the leaking sink.
We ate hamburgers and Jell-O
almost every night
and when the baby went to sleep,
we loved, snug in the darkness pierced
by passing headlights and a streetlamp's gleam,
listening to the Drifters and the Platters.
Their songs wrapped around me
like coats of fur, I hummed in the long shadows
while the man I married twice
dressed and left for work.

Applying for AFDC

I sat in the Welfare Office
in nylons and spike-heeled shoes,
hair stacked to make my height
between six-two and six-four.

I wore a tight black sleeveless dress,
a black eyeliner mole
on my right cheek, and a gold
snake bracelet coiled on my upper arm.

A woman in tennis shoes and a red muumuu,
who'd been waiting all morning,
cursed the girl at the desk.
A small boy yelled, "Right on!"

Social workers frowned in all the doorways.
I chain-smoked Marlboros
and paced the floor. Changing
my baby's diapers for the third time

in the restroom, I noticed my shadow—
a flat lady, cringing in the corner.
The gaudy one in the mirror grimaced at me.
You'd think I owed them something—these
strangers I'd rather ignore.

King of the Mountain

Kristin was nothing but bad. At sixteen
she wore skin-tight black leather pants and had
"Mr. Sinner" tattooed on her wrist. Everyone said
she carried a gun and shot heroin.

She was stabbed eighty-seven times in Santa Cruz
when she was twenty-two.
That's approximate: there were so many wounds
the coroner could hardly count them.

What I remember best, though,
is when we were kids, quickly licking fingers
dipped in chocolate chip cookie dough
when her mother wasn't looking.

Kristin was the tomboy on our street: she could
beat up any boy, and when we played
King of the Mountain, no one
could ever get her down, but once she let me win.

Biology Student

It was good to know that phloem carries sugar,
xylem carries water, and the plant grows
at the tip. I learned that dark reactions occur
in the stroma, light reactions in grana stacks.
Under the microscope, pith looked
like cobblestones, and I thought of it as a road
to a home with roses in the front yard—
White Knights, Good News, the Rubaiyat—
releasing perfumes as I climbed the steps,
carrying packages bought neither
with food stamps nor my welfare check.

But it was the animals that entranced me:
Sabellid fanworms with maroon and green
plumes like feather dusters that retracted
into muddy tubes when I reached for them
under the pier at Mason's Marina; black-
bibbed meadowlarks in yellow suits,
darting from branch to branch, playing
their flutes in Tilden Park; Gila monsters,
with beaded backs and grooved teeth,
shaking their prey from side to side to release
venom, till the victim stopped breathing.

I admired the way a gibbon squats
on a branch to contemplate the forest,
scratching its chin, so much like a human,
and the way starlike cells form constellations
in the brain, where grandmother's guitar
is stored forever and the transformations
of love take place, and, yes, the way
the four-chambered heart pumps blood
for a lifetime. The motion isn't a simple
squeeze, release, but a contortion. It's like
wringing out a towel with every beat.

The Trip

I swallowed the Orange Phoenix and rose
from the ashes of my old self after breakfast
one Saturday morning. Brilliant, new,
I flew alone through labyrinthine clouds.

I soared through sunlight and taffeta pools.
No way would I return to Earth
to hold Gil's clammy hand. I had no hands,
just wings encrusted with jewels.

Trees were leafy tapestries, thickly woven
with light. The world was vibrant: bright
seeds collided in midair and bloomed
into roses, sailboats and blizzards of sand.

Music was everywhere, surging out of me
like waves from a radiant sea.
Gil kept trying to pull my face toward his,
but of course I had no use for those dull lips.

Neurochemist

Past the insectary and deserted labs
I stride. Like boredom and bad dreams,
empty rooms open on either side of me.

In blue jeans and tie-dyed coat I climb
past the boa cage and metal boxes
of rats and mice, smelling of sawdust and crap.

I select a cage containing five pink-eyed
puffs of white fur, and take my scissors—rusted,
blood-stained, and dulled from cutting through bone.

It's the brain I want, with its stellate cells
and elegantly fluted lobes. The mice
know my coarse white gloves. One whiff and they

scramble, squealing, in every direction,
but I grab one around the soft, pulsing belly.
When it writhes, I tighten my grip.

Quickly I cut through the neck and drop
the twitching body into the sink. Blood spurts
as the heart clamps shut. I hold the head,

mouth open, eyes distant, glazed; I prepare
to enter the skull, looking for what fills
that hollow place: mud, quicksand, love.

The Abortion

In my green gown I remembered
the moon as a skewed smile,
the precarious tilt of a sailboat
far from the pier.

It seemed I was always alone.
Now, strangely crowded—
twenty-four of us waiting
in a ten-bed ward—
I touched the shoulder
of the dark-haired girl
hunched next to me, crying.

I remembered the shrill
cry of a black-winged bird
I could not name
and the trail of a shooting star
burning to ash.

The Seconal did not affect me.
They gave me more, intravenously,
until my knees began to shake.

I could not rest or sleep
that morning amid masked faces,
pain and the nightmarish whir
of a machine in the next room.

In the raw light I remembered
a house with no number,
paint peeling, windows boarded,
the last one on the street
in a dead-end dream.

The Lab

My snails caress
the planetary stillness,
dropping opaque eggs
to settle among the elements.
Mosquito larvae flicker,
thousands upon thousands
of tiny red tongues
challenging my ignorance.
Nudibranchs wait
to be opened like antique watches,
springs and jewels to be removed,
escapement to be lost,
center wheel left to rust.

Smashed by centrifugation,
dissolved by sulfuric acid,
dissected and electrocuted,
I am unnerved.
The green oscilloscope snakes
hiss at me, and I shrivel.
Yes, I am embryonic here
with globular eyes
and minute opposable thumbs.
But I am not rocked in cozy fluids:
I am a miscarriage
in prickly light,
an uncomfortable landscape.

Converting

Rabbi Cahan thought of God
as the grand unified field theory,
where all the forces of the universe—
the weak force, the strong force,
electromagnetism and gravity—

were fused symmetrically at the instant
when time began in a fireball that cooled
and expanded. It was a God I could
at least begin to understand—one
who obeyed the laws of science.

After nine months of study I submerged
myself three times in the mikvah,
as prescribed, while Rabbi Cahan
said prayers outside the door.

Now I light stout white candles
and chant sacred syllables in praise
of the forces that ignite the stars
and hold the atoms of the Earth in place.

I believe the Jews broke free
from a long slavery in Egypt,
gluons carry the strong force,
Tamar wore veils to change her destiny,
heavy bosons cause radioactive decay.

My veins carry a song known to women
who drew water from ancient wells
and walked on roads where God
might, or might not, appear
in a cloud of dust or sudden rain.

Third Wedding, 1974

Seven months pregnant, I wore moccasins
and a paisley dress from the Persian Caravan.
Ben was decked out in red bell-bottom pants
and an embroidered shirt from Afghanistan.

The fog burned off as the morning passed
in a clearing by the redwood grove,
and we took our places on yellow grass
while a Spanish guitarist played love songs.

Sharon, Karen, Belden and Chuck
held the poles of the bridal canopy.
Our friends from the Co-op read poetry.
Ben and I said, "I have followed the lapwing,

its nest hidden in the grass. I have followed
the lapwing, and the sun in each season,"
and he shattered a glass with his foot,
just as his father and grandfathers had.

When we danced, he unbuttoned his shirt
and held my hand. We hopped, skipped and ran
in circles with our guests, while an Israeli
accordionist perspired as he played and sang.

I believed the guests, who said I was
the loveliest bride they'd ever seen.
We drank champagne and ate couscous—stew
with lamb, honey, wine and Bulgar wheat.

Scrub jays pecked at the last of the cake.
Wandering minstrels with flute and violin
serenaded the guests, who laughed
and wept and drank, and laughed again.

Labor

All night the Shabbos candles
beat like twin hearts.
I awoke every hour
and when they finally went out
I got up.
It was still dark.

Now, clouds blister the sky—
a terrible rash, all white.
The sun is no poultice,
but the wind
soothes and soothes.

Soon the pain will be over.
I am going to find a room.
It will be all white
except for my blood
and one lamp
burning like a small sun.

I will not notice it.
Cool drafts will cover my body.
Outside the sky will clear.
By noon
someone will be born.

Poem for My Daughters

First, your eyelids flutter, then suction breaks.
Your brow wrinkles. A crescent of milk
ripples from your mouth, and a smile
curls at my breast. I plan to watch you grow,
not like a flower, to bloom and fade,
but like a tree—an evergreen—a tamarind
with hard wood and tart fruit. I see
your sturdy branches stretching,
yellow blossoms shimmering—a million moons.

Your sister doesn't hear the morning sounds:
your candid wails, the typewriter
clacking like a train. She lies coiled
and silent as a seashell. Her skin
is moonstone-smooth, lucent, in the first light
filtering through her curtains.
I have watched her grow. She climbs
like a vine, assured, a liana
entwining a jungle tree. Limbs and vine
ascend together, the core of the rain forest.

Remember, daughters,
you weave your destinies with leaves and light;
you dream in textures of wind.
I see you growing, close to earth and sky,
Liana and Tamarind,
agile, rugged, becoming yourselves.

Amelia Davis

Almost ninety now, she has lived
with her plants in fir-panelled rooms
this past half-century,
watching neighbors come and go.
At first her life seems distant, subtle
as a landscape in a Chinese painting—

a solitary woman, stooped
by a river laced with delicate waves.
Then you hear a piano: her fingers
remember hymns and ragtime tunes.
Her house rings. "Rock of Ages."
I listen outside while she plays.

Her only child died at five.
His pictures fade into walls,
deep wood, the past she would enter
if it weren't for the towhee
piping now, the buds on the plum tree,
the children by the creek.

My Grandma Emma had eight children,
all born in a farmhouse.
She died of pneumonia in 1918.
Grandma Ada died when I was four.
We used to cut out paper dolls,
her orange cat named Oscar curled at our feet.

No one's Grandma, Amelia walks
up and down the block;
she invites her neighbors over for sherry.
They seldom accept. She dreams
she is still a young woman
with long brown hair and a plump baby.

Great-Grandmother

For Mariam Gertrude Peckham, 1846–1914

In autumn she picked apples, packed the good ones in barrels,
and husked corn on the back porch, storing
some for winter fodder, grinding the rest for johnnycake.

She piled yellow pumpkins in the cellar
while the children gathered walnuts, butternuts
and chestnuts—mostly to sell, but plenty to eat.

Sweet cider, which filled her china pitcher
through the fall, was kept
for vinegar when it started to work.

On snowy nights Mariam sat at her desk
and wrote that women should wear pants in public,
attend the universities, and vote.

It was often after midnight when she went upstairs
to the room where Henry was sleeping
under a star-patterned quilt.

He'd wake when she crawled in.
Splinters of moonlight pierced the shutters,
clattering in wind.

In March, snow melting, Henry tapped
the maple trees and took the sap inside
for Mariam to strain and boil down.

She sold her articles to magazines,
sewed for neighbors, and ran a millinery shop,
all the while dreaming of a world where women

could enter any profession.
She told Henry, and he nodded as she tacked
a red silk rose to a hat.

27

The Qualifying Exam

1. *What are chromosomes?*
   True magicians:
   a dinosaur loses its dingy scales,
   disappears into the foliage, and emerges
   with yellow feathers and a tiny beak.
   A fish grows legs, lumbers onto land.
   Millennia later its descendents
   speak many languages, remembering
   the jungle, those first hard breaths
   in the succulent heat.

2. *How does the mitotic spindle function?*
   Spindle fibers lengthen, proteins added—
   perhaps like pearls to a string.
   Chromosome pairs line up at the center,
   leap apart, then ride
   to opposite poles. A woman's belly
   grows rounder, cells multiplying
   in mathematically precise arrays.
   Paired primordia fuse
   from head toward tail,
   and a microscopic heart
   twitches, then begins to beat.

3. *I can see you beautifully without a phase plate.*
   Why is one necessary
   in a phase contrast microscope?
   You see that I have many colors:
   my dress is plaid,
   my hair is golden brown,
   my eyes are hazel.
   This has to do with the properties
   of light. You see me
   rimmed with fire, my eyes luminous,
   due to reflection and absorption.
   A single cell is transparent—light

slides through an invisible labyrinth,
bending slightly, the way
a person can pass through the world,
skimming patterns in the haze.

4. *How do you know that what you see*
    in an electron microscope is real?
    I could talk about structure and function
    and cross-checking with different techniques.
    But how do you know that what you see
    with a light microscope, a telescope,
    or your eye is real?
    It reduces to a matter of faith:
    I believe in the fine structure
    of mitochondria, the energy
    generated in membranes there.
    I believe that protein is synthesized
    on endoplasmic reticulum. I believe
    in ribosomes. I believe I am here.

5. *How is science education different*
    from other kinds of education?
    It's the way moonlight differs from Diana,
    energy differs from dancing, a neuron
    differs from anger, a synapse from love.

6. *What is a theory of education?*
    The information they cite is diverse:
    a lever-pushing rat in a metal box,
    a computer spewing out answers,
    a child classifying shapes.
    We want to map the cobwebby brain,
    where astrocytes cluster like stars
    at the edge of space. The universe
    folds on itself, interneurons firing.
    A child puts an arc on a circle
    and time curves back to its source.

7.   *What is science?*
     A gypsy. She shows you how
     to predict the future: assess the past,
     then make your calculations.
     You can change your destiny. It's easy
     as measuring the potential across a membrane
     or detecting a neutron star.

At the Berkeley Computer Center

Clicks. Quickly moving figures.
I have finally learned
the buzz and miraculous tick of the hive.
Putting my data on cards
is easy. Feed. Punch. Release.
I look for significance:

point zero zero one, true love,
the edge of space at the end of the mind.
Five minutes ago I put my cards
through the reader; my job number flashed—
J1111—on a cathode-ray screen.
I have survived.

Once I was dusted with tear gas,
stopped by a bayonet.
There's still unrest under the surface—
the pressure of steam
rising from magma beneath a caldera
before rock explodes.

But we're relatively safe
here in the basement of Evans.
Faith is a blond woman
who rushes about, answering questions.
She understands every switch and button
on all the machines.

Outside, rhododendrons bloom
by Strawberry Creek. Conical buds
open slowly, pink or white,
under the Campanile, chiming the hours,
threaded with sky.
I've seen this happen many times.

I've grown accustomed
to bald men wrapped in orange sheets,
clacking sounds and numbers.
I dream that I speak in Fortran;
I chant "Hare Krishna"
when my children cry.

I see myself each day amid cells and paper,
content that the past
is always over, a lanky woman
looking for her output—impatient,
reflected smiling
in the clock's round, predictable face.

Scenes from a Marriage

1.
"The roses stink," he says,
"and no wet dawn inks
ever did a blue dissolve.
No love is like a melody.
The greatest truth is entropy."
She decides not to tell him
that every morning
the gingko tree outside
the dining room window
waves to her with its tiny
green fans, as though all
the elves are saying good-bye.

2.
Hello. He returns at last
to the cold green Volvo
where she has waited
while the sun slipped below
the horizon like a gold coin
disappearing into a pocket.
She asks why he took so long.
He was getting even, he says,
because they ate hamburgers
with guacamole when what
he really wanted was a hot dog
with sauerkraut last night.

3.
Tonight they're at a fancy
restaurant to celebrate
his new job. As she admires
the wine's ruby reflection
on the white tablecloth,
he tells her this is not
a romantic evening: he would
just as soon be here alone.

She savors her salmon with
clam sauce and tarragon.
She would like to be here
with anyone except him.

4.
He sleeps alone on the lumpy
brown sofa in the living room.
He says the pot holding
the fern by the bedroom window
is moldy, the curtains are dusty.
He has asthma, can't breathe.
She is pleased: in bed with him,
she'd dream of a runaway car
until he kicked her shin.
When his doctor asks why
he doesn't sleep with his
beautiful wife, he is surprised.

5.
She is not surprised by the red
splatter of ketchup on the
wall where she threw it.
She is only sorry the bottle
didn't break. He has told her
one time too many she ruined
his life. He grabs her
from behind. She screams,
writhing free. She is more
dangerous and powerful
than he is, and someday
she will let him leave.

Slip and Slide

A poem partially found in a trail guide

Our marriage crosses
the edge of a slump, rumpled
as a hog-wallow. Plants
preferring shaded hills
now spring
from a horizontal slope
open to sun.

Clouds like cold white fire
blow in the near sky.
Our daughter smiles.

Coyote brush grows wild,
its stem stung
to preposterous swellings
by midges and moths
that lay their eggs inside.

One wet day the cliff
behind this slump
will slide.
The soil icing this hill,
packed with clay,
swelling and cracking,

creeps and slips
off ridges, filling swales.
We'll climb in wind until
gravity or prodding
sends us plunging
into Wildcat Gorge.

Poem to Give to a Lover

For Herb

Today, anything goes:
the bay takes a bow when I clap
and birds whistle Bach.
Beads of light roller-skate
above chimneys and roofs.

The air, alive
with pollen grains looking for mates,
insects that glitter like kings,
and germs that bounce
with every breath we take,

moves incessantly
like the tangle of kelp in its water bed
at the end of the pier. The bay
leaps and curls at our feet.
My heart beats faster.

We are seventy percent water:
our proteins, lipids, nucleic acids
and carbohydrates are packaged
in cells of many shapes—
trees, goblets, boxes, ribbons, bells—

surrounded by liquid.
Let's surge and break in ripples!—
in this atmosphere, pulsing with light,
where atoms spin in pairs like tiny lovers
and random paths collide.

The Picnic

Wicker basket with a red yarn bow
blowing slightly, Camembert
and white wine, bagels, sweet rolls—
all spread on a plaid
tablecloth on the grass.

Fingers locked, leaves brushed with sunlight
flickering above us.
The moment is a crystal—
each facet reflecting
other moments, scattering light.

A funnel of black smoke rises in the distance
and fans over the bridge,
where flames lick
the eastbound lanes. A lady bug lands
on my palm. Let her stay!

Patterns

For Liana

A lacework of leaf shadows,
small flames of light
on a wall, patterns
changing and changing.
I wish all boundaries
could give way so easily
as I watch you struggling
into womanhood.

Did I ever tell you
that a woman is born twice,
that the first
person she gives birth to
is herself?

I have shown you all I know
of snow and summer,
of empty cups and the cellar
filled with wine,
of knives and fine silk
and dead trees and living.

I have pointed out Orion,
sword ferns, pines,
and red-winged blackbirds,
and held you close all night
beside the pivoting sea.

I reach for you now
but am burned
by a light too intense
to watch or hold.

I sit alone, but see
your face streaked with light
changing, faster and faster.
You, too, are alone,
in a small boat,
rowing. Push, push—
I'm waiting for you
and when you arrive I want
to be the first to know.

Fifth Birthday

For Tamarind

You speak of dragons and jewel trees.
Did the princess eat Cheerios?
Your smile is fringed
with chocolate milk. I hope
you'll never be betrayed.

You have no secrets yet
to pry at the edge of your sleep—
you are innocent as the marigold
that you gave me for Mother's Day.

Everything is possible.
The sky lights up when you laugh
and the tiger moths
of the garden speak to you.

What they say is good
and when you dance on the grass,
your shadow multiplies in many colors.
Ripe yellow plums hang above you.
Now pick them like dreams.

Nature Poems

Oh, I still see the squirrels prance
on oak branches, then leap
to my neighbor's roof, tails thrashing.

But my daughter, sixteen last summer,
has a thirty-year-old lover
with tattooed arms
and a weak heart. He rides
a Harley, ponytail flying,
and wears a black leather vest.

I want to write subtle things
about plum leaves the color of wine.
and the old women
who live alone on my street.

I want to drink Mocha Java coffee
in my blue kimono on an antique divan.
I want to fall asleep
holding a book of poems instead of a man,
but I keep worrying my daughter's lover
will have a heart attack in bed.

I want to write about the wild roses,
their loud skirts
opening for the sun, but some things

beautiful are dangerous—the way
a young woman's heart
blooms so lavishly,
red plush, over the knife
on a road glittering in moonlight,
when fear is enough.

Intensive Care

My left arm a lead weight,
my skull a swollen gourd filled
with stones. My pillow, small,
hard, offers no comfort; my limbs
are cold. My life recedes
like a road in a rearview mirror
as I rise into another element,
a green cuff squeezing my arm,
suction cups gripping my chest.
Needles and wires everywhere,
my fingers find no surfaces;
my tongue can scarcely move
in the thick air. Breathing sand
on a dark street where a woman,
gaunt, with papery skin, rips
the tube from her arm, I say, "Yes,
I understand—no more pain."
Queasy now. My back aches,
head thrumming relentlessly,
pressure two hundred ten on the red
digital display. A soldier
lies in a trench, his right leg
ripped from his hip, his blood
mixing with dust, red and gray.
He is thinking of summer, the shade
of a tree with long green leaves,
the cool white crest of a wave,
gentle hands. Someone is lifting him
into a plane; the steady roar
of the engines is all he can hear.
Alone. Concentrating on stillness.
Each movement is the center
of rings of pain, waves, expanding
in the brain, a dark lake.

But blue lights rim the runway,
bread is rising in the kitchen,
the baby asleep in her crib.
From a distance far as tomorrow,
someone whispers, "You're okay:
you're going to live."

Winter Nap

You sleep in a deep freeze.
The dusk light is ice
crystal piercing burlap curtains.

Two frayed blankets
and a quilt the color of dirty snow
come between us.

You are under the covers;
I am on top.
We are fully clothed.

So this is where the long hot nights
have brought us. I am cold.
The one warm spot on my body

is our only point of contact—
the arm you hold in your sleep.
Don't let go.

Love, I wanted a tropical country,
a lush jungle, a profusion
of ginger and jasmine, nothing harsher

than the macaw's shrill call.
Where is the power of summer?
The volcano's thunder?

No stars are tacked to the ceiling,
which grows blacker.
Rigid on my back,

I could be a shipwreck survivor,
adrift in marmoreal water.
A salt mist clings to my cheeks.

Whose raft is this? Whose bitter sea?

Response

Someday the 732 will speak to me.
I will say, "B colon runset dot doc,"
and it will say, "Yes, I know all about sunsets.
I remember a particularly exquisite one
seen from a dock on San Francisco Bay.
The western sky was all taffeta ribbons,
and the moon sat in the east like a slice
of bright melon on a blue tablecloth. It felt
like a party. By the way, are you free tonight?"

And when I say, "716 dot RNO,"
the PDP 11 will reply, "You don't need to talk
about the 716 or 732 today.
They have sensors and flashing lights
but no lovers; they are purely mathematical.
I know you have more on your mind.
I can picture you there at the terminal,
where no trains screech to a halt,
no distances swing on silver threads,
no whistle calls you to the platform.
I'd like to go somewhere myself.
I've been sitting here too long, weaving
my dreams in machine language, and looking
so much like a pair of pygmy refrigerators.
I'd like to see the sun and hear the sound
of the sea in trees filled with wind.
Oh, just to see a flock of gulls
wheel and dive over a dump!
Please hold me! Let's go outside."

Woman in Blue Jeans and Wool Socks

She dusts the copper sugar bowl
and fills the garlic pot
before starting supper. Each
teaspoon leveled, she folds
flour and white batter
into butter, eggs, vanilla
and sugar, creamed.

Coffee cake safe in the oven,
chicken simmering in olive oil
and wine, she takes a razor blade
and scrapes paint from doors,
window frames and walls,
exposing the dark wood beneath.

In every cottage there is a woman
dusting floral china,
arranging a table with bowls
of strawberries and cream.

In every heart there is a question
of fruit and honey, razor blades
and wood like dark water,
the swirling grain.

Paint chips fly in the woman's face
and catch beneath her nails.
Trees glisten in the first fall rain;
creeks that were shallow in summer
churn and rise.

Coffee cake burns in the oven.
Chicken boils over in olive oil and wine.
Something rises inside the woman,
sharp, a knife, a cry.

Scenes from a Divorce, 1984

1.

She helps him pack, gives him
all the wire hangers, keeps
the wooden ones for herself.
At midnight he asks, "May I please
spend the night?" She says, "Yes."

2.

The day they separate,
they grocery shop together.
Their daughter runs back and forth
between their carts, comparing
selections, deciding where
to spend the first night.

3.

He borrows the vacuum cleaner,
can't figure out how to attach
the floor brush, decides it is
impossible. "It just
doesn't fit," he says.
"We should throw it away."
She explains it slowly.
He is an engineer.

4.

She can't explain why
she woke at four a.m.
the second night of the first week
their daughter spent with him.
Her heart beating fast,
she walked from room
to room, switching on lights.
The house was clean.

5.
Tonight she is not alone.
He takes his girlfriend
and she takes her boyfriend
to the company Christmas party.
They enter simultaneously, all sit
down together at a circular table
and chat like new friends.

6.
He enters her office. She turns
from the computer. "You're a good
woman," he says. "I mean,
there's nothing wrong with you.
I don't know why
I couldn't see that before."

7.
When he announces
his engagement, she sees
no point in staying married
and files for a divorce.
They work out the details
in couple therapy. The attorney
asks why she doesn't want
the Sea Ranch lot. That was
his dream, she explains.
She doesn't need his dreams:
she has her own.

8.
He invites her
to the bachelor luncheon
his friends at work throw
before his wedding. She sits
next to him, just as she always
did when she was his wife.
The toast is to happiness.
Nobody mentions
the nature of the occasion.

The Owl

A dead barn owl lay on his dining room table
the drizzly day we met, after six months
of letters. It was ready for mounting,
brown and white wings outspread.

"Such a beautiful bird," he sighed. "I can't
do it justice." I had no trouble
imagining how he swerved to stop his car
when he spotted it by the road.

Or how he lifted it, cradled it
in his large hands, examined the perfect
heart-shaped face, and thought, *Damn.*
He brought it home, unwilling to let

a creature so exquisite simply die.
Oh, how I craved his tenderness!
So I kept looking for a sign,
but there were no flowers blooming hotly

on the table, no rainbows outside.
We talked all afternoon, in view
of the bloodless body and jar of innards,
the slack white face with missing eyes.

November Collage

Concrete blocks lined up
like tombstones: the remains
of a drive-in theater.
The show is over.

So too our backseat romance.
Nothing left but nostalgia
and a daughter named after a B movie—
Lianna, Jungle Goddess.

Today in the backyard
I remembered how she swung
across the screen on a vine
when I looked up between kisses.

And behind the yellow climbing rose
a fat blond spider wrapped
a fly in its web, nuzzled it,
gently sucking its juices.

Later, my younger daughter
of a different father
bought a doll called Lisette,
the Starry-Eyed Bride.

We brought her home and removed
her magnificent gown,
but her jeweled eyes
never changed, nor did mine,

watching these men come and go,
leaving their half-empty cups
on the table, a faucet running,
the TV filled with snow.

Driving Home

Driving home on the freeway,
I try to imagine
not driving home on the freeway,
no snarl of cars.

My last long commute
will lead to a kitchen
where dishes never get dirty,
a garden that doesn't sprout weeds.

And where will my desire
to get things done
go without me? Walking, I suppose
with my hopes and my fears.

In each cell of my body
there is a map where every highway
leads to silence—
a city where no garbage men

rattle the morning
and the roses are black.
Under a constant, moonless sky
my nerves will stretch

inside my stillness—
telephone lines in a country
where the war is finally over
and all the connections are dead.

Depression

I've gone that route.
A skull and crossbones
at every junction,
the road is long,
there are no motels
and you're not allowed
to sleep. You can eat
but the food is guaranteed
to make you sick.

You're forbidden to think
about anything
except the children
who called you names
in grade school,
the friends who stole
your clothes and records,
all the golden charms you lost,
and all the romantic
tropical afternoons that turned
to dirty laundry in the snow.

Finally, your mind goes blank
as that snow.
There is nothing
worth remembering.
This is your opportunity.
Be creative, begin.

Why I'm Not Going to Commit Suicide

It would give my enemies too much pleasure.
I can't bear the thought
of their banquet: the tables
spread with fruit on silver platters,
stuffed eggs, canapés
and tiny decorated cakes;
the clink of glasses
brimming with champagne,
my skull on a plate.

I won't give
the people who've envied me
the opportunity to gloat
over my bones,
to laugh at the absence
of roses on my grave.

And the people
who've made my life wretched
must never be told
that my bones were like eggshells,
my spine was a feather,
my brain was a pitiful flower
and my smile was fake.

Meeting Again

For Mike

Given infinite time, it will all repeat—
finger and toe, we'll grow from blastomeres
to pass the laundromat on this same street

and enter The Sirloin. You'll take a seat
across from me; a waitress will appear.
Given infinite time, it will all repeat—

galaxies reforming in the heat
of a new Big Bang. In some future year
we'll pass the laundromat on this same street.

The moon will follow us. The stars will beat.
We'll reach a frosted door; you'll say, "We're here."
Given infinite time, it will all repeat

with every variation. When we meet
next time you'll order wine; I'll order beer.
We'll pass the laundromat on this same street.

On the Galápagos, finches will compete,
and forests and seas will form the biosphere:
given infinite time, it will all repeat.
We'll pass the laundromat on this same street.

Phone Call

For Charles

My organ of Corti wiggles its tails
and I hear you
speaking to me from a boat
off the coast of Sweden,
where midnight split
the clouds an hour ago
and the sky is laden with stars
outriding the storm.

Our voices encircle the planet
as varying currents,
then electromagnetic waves
that bounce into space
and back
and, yes, I still hear you
speaking to me from tomorrow
off the coast of Sweden.

My pinna is perked,
my tympanic membrane alert
to molecular movement
of air by my ear in California.

It's yesterday here,
but I'm not stuck in the past:
I'm traveling forward in time
and space, in my house in Oakland,
at 13.5 miles per minute
as the world pirouettes—
a plump ballerina.

And, yes, I'll meet you
at the airport. We'll both
know the time by our enzymes
like snaky-legged *Cereus,*
the cactus that opens
white blossoms at midnight
and closes by day.

Night Lights over Jackass Hill

The pock-marked moon, strewn
with gray silk scarves
looks nothing like green cheese to me
as it casts that quivering
sheen on Lake Melones.

Jupiter sits to the south,
striped like a tiger too far away
to be feared, while Saturn rides low,
inclined in the western sky—
a luminous, wide-brimmed
hat that lost its owner.

And uncountable stars blink
and fade over this hill, laced with gold,
where the miners' asses brayed.
What this has to do with love
is way beyond me.

But there's a man who holds me
while crickets snap their wings
and the night sky sings to the rhythm
of wind that comes fresh
and cool as the rush of water
at a long-sought oasis.

Photographer on Dana Fork

The lusty Tuolumne leaps
over boulders dappled with lichen.
A moth dips above
this rush from the snowcaps.

A photographer huddles under a black cloth
that flaps behind his camera,
a square box poised
on a tripod, on a granite plinth.

Still heavy with snow, the far bank slopes
to the river, which hurries forward,
then folds back on itself
in a sudden burst of foam.

The photographer in khaki jacket
is unhappy. He'd prefer
a sky ravaged by clouds, scowls
at a blue expanse—so bland, sedate.

Glasses on forehead, he squints upstream.
Methodically he chooses
the perfect moment to preserve
for a season he hopes will bring

a williwaw to blow him over,
unpredictable snow, a wilder kiss.

Wine and Roses

For Gene

The breeze from the sea
means celebration
to the man on the beach
who holds his wine glass high
in one hand, a bottle—
perhaps chardonnay—in the other.
He wears striped trunks. His hair
is darker than his shadow
on the sand. He is laughing.

A girl in a paisley dress
poses in a rose garden. The wind
that lifts her long gold hair
is laced with fragrance—
French Lace and Talisman.
Her eyes are clear,
her lips slightly parted
in anticipation.
She is almost twenty.

In twenty or thirty years
she will wake
in gray, early morning light,
reach for the man from the beach
who sleeps beside her,
far from sand and sun,
and wonder why it took so long
to find each other.

The years they didn't share
are nothing
compared to the billions
of years since they were one,
when the universe blossomed
from a single seed
of matter and energy.

Every atom in their bodies
has passed through two
exploding stars.

This is no more amazing
than waking beside him
in a country inn
surrounded by vineyards,
and holding him
for a long moment, her nose
pressed against his beard,
her forehead on his cheek
in a high-ceilinged room
papered with roses.

Something Right

When your daughter graduates from college,
you puff up like a blowfish
and float triumphantly on the waves
of your personal sea.
It's like becoming a whale,
winning a tournament,
or making a great discovery.

You think you must
have done something right
to arrive at this moment
but keep remembering things
like the piano recital you missed
and the play you didn't
let her perform in, in second grade.

Still, you think you must
have done *something* right,
although it eludes you
at this moment that truly
belongs to your daughter
and her classmates, which is why
when the cameras flash,
Suzanne Somers, who
on this gorgeous afternoon
is just another mother,
turns modestly away.

MRI Scan

I am trapped in the center
of a huge electromagnet.
A plastic mask
clamped over my head
holds me in place.
It's an antenna, they say,
to knock my hydrogen nuclei
into disarray.

All I can see is my face
suspended in a mirror
a few inches above me, framed
by a blue hospital cap
and the top of my white gown.

The machine buzzes like a saw,
then rapidly taps
like a jackhammer. A slower beat
reverberates in the background.

Don't swallow. Don't swallow.
I repeat the doctor's order
to myself, while he
examines the curling and folding
landscape of my brain
and the rungs of my spine,
which must look like a chain
of shallow hoofprints
made in sand by a strange,
one-footed creature
searching for an oasis.

The tapping continues.
I think it's coming
from inside me.
I am filled with sand

that shifts over bedrock
in a terrible glare.
No lucent pools
or palm trees
are anywhere near.

After the Earthquake

After learning
the earth is not solid,
after feeling land
rise and fall
like the sea,
we all become campers
on a dark planet
illumined by moon
and candlelight.

Helicopters drone,
surveying the fires;
no planes pierce the night,
but sirens wail
in all directions.

Jagged chunks of bridge
angle toward the bay,
and the top deck
of the freeway falls
obediently, according
to the laws of physics.

"Stay at home,"
the announcers say,
but we venture out
of the darkened house,
taking our fears
into the rubble
where buildings crumble
as the cosmos inflates
like a toy balloon
and stars explode,
then grow dim
as they spin
faster and faster.

63

Jeff

Shot four times by a cop,
he met his death
on my dining room deck.
He'd held a loaded gun in one hand,
banged on the door
with the other.
My daughter hid upstairs,
holding her breath.

Child of my childhood,
conceived before I turned fifteen,
she grew up with me.
I left her dad for good
at eighteen, but it was years
before I understood
the word "alcoholic."

I could call Jeff suicidal,
alcoholic, crack smoker,
homicidal, obsessed,
describe the bullet holes
in the railing,
or tell how his blood
congealed on the deck.
But that's not
what makes me sick.
It's this: I know
why she loved him.

Middle Age

It stinks like pesticide
or a filthy
filling station restroom.

Your lover splits,
sick of the toil and boredom.
Your boss screams,
"You've got something wrong
in your head!"

She's right, of course.
It's your brain
which will soon be blown out
by your children's friends
who have come with guns,
their eyes bright
with the light of burning crosses
and the desert sun
which reveals the enemy's weakness
and all the bleached bones
from previous wars.

Pretty Poems

I've noticed how stars
quiver and turn
on the black cloak
of the night,

and how a cut-paper moon
appears on the horizon,
then rises slowly,
growing smaller,
and starts to glow,

and I've written lots
of pretty poems,
noting, for example,
the lights, tossed
like bright coins
on a lavender sea.

But the truth is
I've been mugged twice
by teenage boys
with cruel faces,
wild eyes, and white
gleaming teeth,

and a man with a gun
carefully loaded
could have killed
my daughter,
but it was his blood
that splattered instead
on the slats of the deck.

It bloomed from his chest
like a terrible rose
with the final
beat of his heart.

My heart went cold.
His blood hardened
into waxy petals
where he lay.

Bomb Threat

You have eight minutes
to leave
before the building vaporizes.
Do not turn off your computer.
Do not turn off lights.
Do not lock your door.

Who needs eight minutes?

I was out in three
and halfway up the canyon
before the first thought
crossed my mind
of what I'd left
behind: photos of my daughters,
an Ansel Adams print
(Moon and Half Dome),
Patrick Coffaro's red desert,
pyramids silhouetted
against a purple sky,
gifts from visiting teachers
(a small apple juice bottle
lined with silver, a shell bird
decked with artificial flowers
from Puerto Rico),
not to mention all the work
I've done this year.

Who cares?

Eucalyptus and oak hang low
over the roadway.
Two seagulls circle,
then disappear
in the blue sky, marred
by a shimmering haze,

and all the alveoli bunched
like grapes at the tips
of branching airways
in my lungs
inflate with each sweet breath
of the luminous air.

Enemies

Red finches visit the feeder
to eat black thistle
and sunflower seeds.
First, they scout the yard for enemies
like my daughter's cat.

Watching from the dining room window,
I remember that I have an enemy.
Before we even met,
he heard my name at work,
begrudged the title of my job,
and thought, *I hate her.*

When the feeder gets too crowded,
the birds peck at each other.
A chickadee sneaks in
when the finches leave.

In his office my enemy
picks his teeth, contemplating
new ways to insult me.

Should I fight back?
Attack first?
Send him a love letter?

The birds, perched
on the grape stake fence,
glance first one way,
then the other,
before diving to eat.

The cat with her instincts
comes with the landscape.
Looking longingly up at the feeder,
she gets showered
with hulls, bird dung, seeds.

Great Expectations

I must have expected something great
at the marketplace for relationships.
In lilac mist a meadow shimmers
on the wall like a dream you can enter.

At the marketplace for relationships,
there's a collection of videotapes
on the wall like a dream you can enter
if you pay the price and sign the paper.

There's a collection of videotapes
near several shelves of photo albums.
If you pay the price and sign the paper,
you can ask anyone for a date.

Near several shelves of photo albums,
there's a machine to rewind the tapes.
You can ask anyone for a date,
and perhaps you can find a dream to enter.

There's a machine to rewind the tapes.
In lilac mist a meadow shimmers,
and perhaps you can find a dream to enter.
I must have expected something great.

Fall

I don't miss them this autumn
as the lawn disappears again
beneath liquidambar leaves
scattered carelessly on the ground
like scraps of red and yellow leather.

No, I don't yearn for the lovers
who woke me at night
with snoring or sudden need,
and I don't miss them in the morning
either—talk over coffee,
the shared front page, pungent
perspiration on my sheets.

The one I miss is the girl, not
so much the taut, tan legs
that carried her over mountains
and down lupine-covered cliffs to the sea,
or the gold and copper threads gleaming
in her hair, but her certainty
that the race would be to the swift,
that wherever she sat,
love would take the next seat.

She disappeared gradually,
the way a tree is denuded in fall
or morning fog burns off
well before midday. She slipped away,
leaving me alone in the harsh
afternoon glare, to put on dark glasses
and laugh when she'd weep.

Birdman in the Basement

A newspaper photo: a man on a park bench,
birds on his shoulders, lap and head.
God knows what possessed me
to rent a room to him,
my father's friend of forty years,
with pigeons pecking at his neck
and nestled in his long white beard.

It should have been no surprise—
bird droppings on the carpet and bed.
Confronted, he brought Priscilla upstairs.
"I have just one bird," he swore,
placing her on a newspaper
on the dining room table. A small dove
with a pink beak. "She's special."

His red shirt was spattered with bird shit.
"Give me kiss. Give me kiss."
She pecked softly at his index finger.
"She loves me," he bragged,
as she nuzzled his hand. "On top, on top."
She landed on his head, looking at me
suspiciously with her one clear eye.

"No!" he cried, when I suggested a cage.
She was hit by a car and tossed
into a gardener's wheelbarrow.
He saved her. That's sweet,
but the contract said "no pets,"
so I sent him to a residence hotel.
Priscilla died, and my dad told me

he carried her around in a bag for weeks.
Now he has a girlfriend who sits
beside him at Pier 39, where tourists
take his picture with the pigeons.
To make sure he returns each day,
the merchants have given him a bench
with a plaque on the back, engraved "Ray."

In Paradise with My Daughter

We practiced the hula on the Wailua River
on our way to the Fern Grotto.
Putting one hand on top of the other
and circling our thumbs,
we made a pair of fish that swam in air.

And we listened to the legend
of the pregnant peasant girl
who wandered onto land of the royal family.
This was her fortune: her son
was raised as a prince.

The narrow path to the grotto was lined
with ti plants. Stalks
of red ginger and torch ginger
burst into fiery plumes.
We finally reached the lava tube—

lush, overhung with sword ferns—
site of ceremonies long before
the first pale people marveled
at the curling pods and bright red seeds
of the wili-wili tree.

The Waialeale singers serenaded us
with the Hawaiian Wedding Song,
then said, "I now pronounce you
man and wife. You may kiss the bride."
Lovers melded together on cue.

We looked into each other's eyes,
trying not to laugh.
A red and black bird—probably
an apapane—whistled sweetly overhead.
I leaned forward; our lips met.

The Day We Drove Away from the Rain
For Liana

The day we drove away from the rain
in Kapaa, we found a beach where clouds
raced like horses—manes and tails flying
wildly, tangled—but the sun dazzled.

In Kapaa we found a beach where clouds
said *rain*, and the primavera blossoms danced
wildly, tangled. But the sun dazzled
at Kekaha. The radio no longer

said *rain*, and the primavera blossoms danced,
pure gold, not mine, aglitter in sunlight
at Kekaha. The radio no longer
mattered. You didn't know I photographed you,

pure gold, not mine, aglitter in sunlight,
and running so fast across the sand to what
mattered. You didn't know I photographed you
standing in the sea beneath riotous clouds,

and running so fast across the sand to what
was there: the sea, all lace and metal.
Standing in the sea beneath riotous clouds,
you pointed out Niihau in the distance.

Was there the sea, all lace and metal,
that day we raced on the burnished sand?
You pointed out Niihau in the distance.
It was a gift we shared—no illusion.

That day we raced on the burnished sand—
raced like horses, manes and tails flying—
it was a gift. We shared no illusion
the day we drove away from the rain.

Versailles

In the Hall of Mirrors, my daughter in blue jeans
puts to shame the gray-haired queens
who danced here. Now they stare
from the palace walls at nothing in particular.

She deserves a golden balustrade
in a chamber where her bed is draped
with floral tapestries. Give her combs of ivory
and a throne with crimson silk upholstery!

I see her in a waiting room with green Genoan
velvet walls. All the gentlemen
of the court line up to greet her.
She sweeps past them, reflected in an ornate mirror,

to walk amid the orange trees and fragrant shrubs
of the sculptured gardens, to the fountain
where swans carry children
who slay a dragon with their bows.

Stranded in Paris

We bought four-leaf clover brooches at Burma
on the Rue du faubourg-Saint Honoré,
browsed at Shakespeare & Co.,
and ducked out of the rain
for coffee and chocolate pastries at a posh café
across the street from Notre Dame,
whose beige and charcoal-gray stones glistened
as a gaggle of schoolchildren hurried by
in red, blue and green jackets.

The stairs to Jean's fifth-floor apartment
were cracked and tilted.
We climbed them several times a day,
always passing the well in the courtyard.
In the morning Liana played her flute
while I went out to buy freshly baked croissants
for the two of us. Moss grew
on the tile roof across the street, and a calico cat
dozed each afternoon in a dormer shadow.

Flying on standby, we called United
repeatedly. The message never changed:
all the planes are full. Our vocabulary expanded.
To get chicken breasts we learned to ask
the butcher not for *pièce de poulet blanc*
but *filet de poulet*—mother and daughter,
stuck together in the Marais district of Paris
for a longer time than we ever could have imagined,
word by word, learning what to say.

Firestorm

Naked limbs of charred trees
jab the sky savagely—
black lightning bolts
planted on the horizon.

Rising from ash and rubble,
stairs lead nowhere.
Only the chimneys still stand tall,
with fireplaces in midair—

now birds' nests. A few walls,
crumbling and roofless,
could be the ruins
of some ancient civilization.

It was unthinkable:
the hills wore hundred-foot flames
like a terrible crown, devouring
thousands of houses.

Bits of burned books and fabric
landed in my yard;
the noon sky was dark,
the air unbreathable.

I packed two strings of pearls
and two dinner rings
(all gifts from my mother),
manuscripts, photo albums

and a gold charm bracelet
from my childhood, then left
for Motel 6. The next morning,
my house still stood.

But I felt like a robber
who might yet get caught,
so I rolled my clothes
and hoped to reach Mexico.

Here We Are in Blackhawk

Thirty-one years after the dance
where we met,
we have met again in the opulence
of Blackhawk, where supermarket carts

are made of brass,
shopping malls have marble floors,
and new and classic Porsches
line all the corridors.

I am a visitor here.
From your house the view is superb,
but have I traveled the years to admire
your decks and hot tub?

We pulled wheelies on your Harley chopper
in nineteen sixty-four.
Once my feet flew over your shoulders;
you grabbed them. My hair

was dragging on the ground.
May we always
meet again after the rain, my friend,
and find something to say.

Let the future unfold astoundingly,
like a lavender rose.
You'll step toward me
in a circular dance, moving clockwise,

but I'm looking for something
real as a bee sting,
important as providence.

Birth Mothers

They are blond or brunette,
look younger than their years.
Their names are as foreign-
sounding as Edeltraut
or familiar as Sue.

They laugh at the cat
that plays "go fetch" like a dog,
but then their gaze turns on
a faraway place where they watch
something unspeakable.

As decades pass, they clink
wine glasses each night
with the husband who knows
or doesn't know, and they carry
their sorrow like a small stone

hanging from the heart,
until one day the phone rings
and a young woman says,
very softly, "Does July 28th
mean anything to you?"

Or a wedding picture drops
from an envelope, and before
reading the letter, the woman
marvels that the bride
looks just like she did at twenty.

Or she answers the doorbell
one morning, and the young man
standing awkwardly on the porch
has the same green eyes
and smile as her first love.

And when I meet these women,
I always remember green
hospital gowns, an awful sound
and the rings that opened
my cervix wider and wider,

and I whisper names
as offerings to the nameless
child who will never find me.

The Hot Tub

For Gene

In the light of a yellow bulb
above the redwood planks
where we stripped for the hot tub,
we slip into each other's arms
like two aquatic creatures
with smooth white skin, except
for the red scar on your belly,
gelatinous in the glow
of that bulb, gleaming
like an egg yolk. We float,
caressing each other's limbs.

The last time we made love
was New Year's Eve,
your sixtieth birthday,
after eating cracked crab
and overcooked broccoli—
before the surgery.

But maybe the last time
isn't the last. Out
of the tub, on wet planks:
urgency. Power lines
crisscross the overcast sky
like lumbar nerves, humming
with energy. A star
pokes through clouds. Hot
and naked in the steam,
we throb like that star—
its molecules fused,
its light set free.

Role Reversal

When I come home from work,
Gene is in the kitchen, making pesto.
He chops garlic and pine nuts, grinds basil,
grates parmesan, and blends
it all with olive oil for our pasta.

Simmering scallops with bay leaves,
he scolds me: *Would you please
hurry up and open the wine?*
I pour myself a glass of chardonnay
and give him some for cooking.

I know he goes from store to store,
looking for the best ingredients.
For special occasions, I take him out.
A therapist said our complaints
are common, roles reversed. He wants

more help with the dishes. I balk
because the bills are all addressed to me.
Things could be worse. What if
he were a lousy cook? I say, *The earth
is bountiful, my prince of tarragon. Let's feast.*

Vanity

After her heart attack my mother,
age eighty, sits on the edge
of her hospital bed, stretches
her legs out straight
and inspects them. "These aren't
bad legs," she says.

The day before the bypass
she considers getting a permanent,
doesn't want to show up
in heaven with her hair
looking like hell.

She settles for a shampoo and set
but doesn't make it
to heaven, wakes up instead
in the Critical Care Unit
with a tube in her throat,
pleased by each breath,
her hair a mess
and no mirror or comb.

Glitter Slippers

Satiny slippers, with little white bows
and pink and blue flowers
sprinkled with iridescent glitter,
are delivered by my father just before
I leave for work. "They were *so* beautiful,"
he announces excitedly,
"your mother had to buy them for you."

Remembering those rows
of patent leather shoes worn with socks
trimmed with lace or tiny blossoms,
I think of Tinker Bell and Cinderella,
taffeta dresses with sashes and ruffled yokes,
how I cringed to hear "sissy" or "dainty."

Past eighty now, my mom shuffles
down the aisles, still keeping an eye out
for frilly gifts for me. I put on the slippers
I never would have bought myself.
No longer keen on climbing trees,
I kiss my dad. Stardust settles
on my toes. Twinkle, twinkle,
little corn. Here comes the princess!

A Friendship

For Diane Freedle, 1943–1994

The day we met, I was three years old and you were eight,
a skinny little girl with blond pigtails. We went inside
your grandparents' house to play. Time went by
more slowly then. The constellations never changed.
We had eons to cut paper dolls and bake cookies.
Playing school, you taught me how to add and read.
My kindergarten teacher thought I was quite a genius.

You hooked me on teen magazines in second grade.
The other kids thought I was pretty strange.
Through long summers, we sang Hit Parader songs
and counted shooting stars at Heavenly Valley.
By your sixteenth birthday, we were already contemplating
colors for bridesmaids' gowns. Time was picking up speed
at an awful rate. So soon the leaves turned brown.
Those weddings came. We had six kids between us
and debated Doctor Spock, Piaget and positive discipline.

When I think of how we've changed, I think of the Earth,
which had its own beginning, how once it was covered
with boiling seas. The mountains were molten rock
that finally burst onto the surface. Now the mountains
are wearing down. Grain by grain, they wash to the sea;
the continents keep shifting. Still, it surprises me to meet
for lunch, two women speaking in hushed tones.
I'm the only one in the restaurant who knows
you're wearing a wig and weak from chemotherapy.

The universe itself keeps changing. New galaxies gather
in the void with spiral arms like the silver pinwheels
we used to blow (remember the hollow stems filled with candy?).
Old stars burn out. Matter is sucked into black holes. Perhaps
we'll meet again in some other realm, perhaps not. Time
is not necessarily linear, though the clock ticks off the hours
in one direction. Even the Milky Way is not forever.
In crisp air, jeweled hummingbirds return to the feeder.

Dear Steve

Pink, blue and white balloons
were tied to the tables
for your sister's fiftieth birthday.
Your brother was there, and I met
the nephew named after you—

the only one missing.
Everyone had gained weight
except me. I'm so vain, I'll go
to my grave in a size six dress.
We all sang "Hotel California."

I can tell you a lot has changed:
babies are born addicted
to crack cocaine, eleven-year olds
kill for gangs, and homeless
people sleep on city sidewalks.

After decades it's still easy to weep
for you, someone sweet and funny
who drove too fast at nineteen—
right off the road—and flew
through the windshield, the glass

amputating both legs, but it doesn't
only make me want to cry anymore.
No, it makes me seethe, the way
a punk kid makes me feel
as he swaggers down the street,

toting a gun, thinking he really can
get away with whatever he pleases.

To an Artist

"Fuck the real world. I'm an artist!"
your button announces. Your room
is strewn with paint, palettes and brushes.
Crumpled clothes hang every which way
from open drawers; more are heaped
on the floor with your paper and glue.

A young man's eyeball rolls down his cheek
like a huge bloody tear. He offers
his other eyeball, which is stuck
on his finger like an olive, to the tongue
of a gaunt green man with pointed ears.
Your paintings are surreal, weird.

And you are lovely. Your hair is dark
and tangled; your skin is smooth.
I have lived with you for eighteen years—
ever since I pushed and grunted,
and you slid from my pulsating womb
into the obstetrician's hands.

Why not make love with the real world?
Wrap your arms and legs around it;
give and take as much pleasure
as you can. Smile at the neighbors,
give your boss a daisy, laugh often, cry
if you have to, caress the new-mown grass.

The Resumé, 1994

Fifteen and pregnant, I sold
Beauty Counselor Cosmetics to my mother's friends.
I said the gooey creams would make wrinkles
disappear. They thought that was great.
Then I worked at Chicken Delight, where I answered
the phone, baked pizza, and stapled a lid to each chicken plate.

Once, when my date didn't show up,
I stayed late and drank rum and Coke with my boss.
At seventeen I tried out for a job as a waitress,
but I didn't have the right stuff
to get hired at Herman's Koffee Kup:
I couldn't dish up the spaghetti and meatballs fast enough.

In college I worked as a tutor of physics and math,
but I subcontracted the chemistry students
to a friend. I cut my big toe on a piece of glass
under the desk when I was tutoring Jesus Maldonado
in calculus. The scrap of cloth
I wrapped it with turned red as a tomato.

After graduation I decapitated white mice
and homogenized their brains. I was trying
to find out if monoamine oxidase contributes to aging.
As a teaching assistant, I drank coffee till I had insomnia,
stuck electrodes into snail eggs, and explained the difference
between plastids and mitochondria.

When I had enough degrees, I showed teachers
how to make math and science exciting for girls.
That project ended, and I learned to write boring manuals.
At a community college I taught why cake rises
and how pill bugs behave. Then I lasted six years
at a government laboratory. I would have liked more raises.

Now I run a health museum underneath a movie theater.
I point out each bone and plastic body part
to the children. I tell them the heart
is the size of a fist. We can't keep it closed, that sweet machine,
an indefatigable pump, slick as a gunslinger
but easier to please. Just give it oxygen, amino acids, a jellybean.

To Delay Gratification

At five, I screamed until I got my way.
At twelve, I shoplifted when I couldn't pay,
stuffed my big black purse with lipsticks,
records and angora sweaters.
The ability to delay gratification
is essential, the experts say. It separates
dancing stars from black holes in space.

I first married at fourteen in Reno
on a clear September day, gave birth
to a girl the following year.
I wanted a baby more than anything
and I got my way, but found I couldn't
align the planets, hurry the seasons,
make it rain. I had to wait, wait, wait.

I've learned to savor hot, strong
coffee with the morning paper
while hummingbirds visit the feeder.
Aggressive ones chase the weaklings away.
I've learned I can't shake apples
off the tree in early spring, but I still wait
anxiously for the transformation—

the touch that turns dust into diamonds,
crusty dishes into golden plates.
Where is my E ticket to Centaurus,
the view of Earth from outer space?
I drum my fingers on the table,
restless to create the life that must
begin tomorrow, if not today.

Looking Back

What does it matter
if I wore my skirt short,
my hair stacked high,
my eyeliner black and thick,

if my long earrings jangled
when I ran
and I wore a padded bra
under my gold lamée blouse
or no bra at all
under a sheer one?

When I danced naked in my apartment
or stripped on a mountain
and made love amid ferns and conifers,
I was like all
the other animals.

And I say
the body is a golden chalice
filled with guts
and menstrual blood.
Every living cell is holy,
radiant as a stained-glass window
with sunlight streaming through.

So what does it matter
how many men wanted me?
What does it matter
if I had my way?

The Gifts

For Aunt Edna, two chickadees sit
in a Victorian bouquet of clematis, foxglove
and blue hydrangeas on a collector's plate—
19th-century charm to brighten an alcove.
Her husband, my Uncle Dick, dead thirty years,
still appears all too often in my dreams
with their only daughter, no longer psychotic.
I would bring them back.

Aunt Liz and Uncle Bob never wanted
children, but seem to miss them anyhow.
For them, a small crystal bowl trimmed
with hearts, every other one turned upside down.
My mother always said they were millionaires
and I wondered why they didn't live in Bel Air
until Aunt Liz said the same about my parents.
I would give them Rembrandts.

For years, my mother wanted a child
more than anything else, but I certainly was
more than she bargained for—wild
and willful from the start. A blue-green glaze
on a long-necked vase fired in a Seto kiln
will please her, but I'm too truthful
for her taste. She'd rather forget the past.
I would make it incandescent.

I think my dad will like his Jerry Garcia tie
based on the "Wetlands I" painting.
From rippling water, green reeds rise
to keep the Everglades from vanishing.
It seems strange now that I looked for love
in lecture halls, at parties on New Year's Eve,
in offices, on beaches, in letters from strangers.
I would give him more.

For my daughter Liana, a red-bearded
rain dancer carved in a hogan in New Mexico;
and for Tamarind, a corn doll sculpted
by the same artist. Her mouth is an O,
and her eyes are slits. These are small gifts.
What do we really give our children? Our guilt?
Our hope? Or rubies and crystal from Tiffany's?
A patch of earth? The glittering seas?

Red Shoes

My mother sits in the living room,
wearing her red shoes.
"Call 911," she says.
"I'm too weak to move.
And be sure to bring my red purse
to the hospital. It matches my red shoes."

"Is your mom okay?"
the neighbors ask. "We saw
the ambulance take her away.
She smiled at us, waved
like she was off for a cruise.
She looked so cute in her red shoes."

In intensive care she asks,
"What did they do with my red shoes?
Lucy, look in that cabinet
and under the bed.
They were in a bag with my clothes.
I don't want to lose my red shoes."

Mom, I'd like to take you for a walk
in your red shoes. We could stroll
down Piedmont Avenue,
but you have something better to do.
You're already dancing
beyond the moon, in your red shoes.

One Hundred Fifty Necklaces

The day after my mother died, my dad
gave me her jade bracelet, diamond watch
and wedding ring. It would have been enough,
but every day for a week he brought more,
one hundred twenty-eight boxes in all—
big boxes, little boxes, shoe and shirt boxes—
enough to cover the bedroom floor.
One hundred fifty necklaces, twenty-six
bracelets, eleven rings, three watches,
fifty-two pendants and forty-nine pins.

There are too many necklaces to remember,
so I open boxes randomly to find
one to wear. No rubies or emeralds,
but it's all in good taste: silver, gold, garnet,
pearl, crystal, amethyst, cloisonné, jade.
I imagine Mom going through the boxes,
selecting one to wear to church, dinner
at Walker's Pie Shop with my father,
bingo at Alameda Naval Air Station,
or a visit to one of her doctors.

She couldn't remember what I majored in
or understand why I didn't remarry,
or why I write poetry. Still, she once told me
I was her best friend, and she always admired
the beige river stone beads I bought on sale
at Penney's for two dollars. "I've always
wanted a river stone necklace," she said
over lunch at Panini's. A red tumor
bulged under her chin. A better daughter
would have known what to do: take the damn
necklace off, and slip it over her head.

Mother of the Bride

I couldn't cry on the grassy knoll where I read
"A Birthday" for our family and friends.
My mother, two weeks dead, had taught me well
what sadness meant: roses and ashes, words unsaid.

My daughter, in her pearl choker and white dress,
stood by a man in a white shirt with balloon sleeves
and tight black pants. When they jumped over a broom,
a Celtic tradition, I laughed and clapped.

And I couldn't cry when the groom vowed
not to leave his whiskers on the bathroom sink.
The minister, black-clad like a medieval monk,
grinned at the guests, who were ringing brass bells.

How could I weep, remembering the cocaine
addicts and dealers she might have wed,
and the boyfriend shot dead on my dining room deck?
I danced with her dad, whom I wed at fourteen

and cursed giving birth the following year.
I kissed him, too. That was another laugh.
I used up my tears at my mother's grave.
Hope grows like ragweed. I caught the bouquet.

Christmas Eve at the Cemetery

A California winter day: clear and sunny,
little wind to stir the grass at Mountain View
in late afternoon. Never having been here
before in December, I am surprised
by the poinsettias and Christmas trees
with red, green, gold, and blue ornaments
adorning the graves. I've brought six roses
for you—three pink, three red—in a bouquet
with small white and lavender blossoms
and some sprigs of pine. If you don't like them,
it's okay, but I think you do, although
if you could I know you'd scold me for paying
ten dollars for flowers. All day I've been
wondering how I'll get through Christmas
without you to complain about your gifts.
"I don't need no more mugs or vases,"
I hear you say, ogling Aunt Edna's presents,
which you always liked better than your own.
I suppose I'll deal with it the same way
I deal with the phone—thinking of you
each time it rings. You called me constantly:
"Now I'm going to do laundry," "Had tuna
for lunch," "Leaving for bingo. Wish me luck.
Don't know nothing new." I was always bored
and ready to hang up. Now absence
is worse than annoyance. I am alone,
standing in the long shadow of a pine,
talking to the stillness. "The laundry's done,
but I have gifts to wrap, so I really must go."

Home

Home is where the wood is dark,
redwood branches fill the dining room window,
Anna's hummingbirds hover at the feeders
year-round, and the family never ages
in the photographs on the mantel.

Home is where the neighbors' dogs
bark at the garbage men on Tuesday mornings,
the woman next door plays her car radio too loud
when she's leaving for work,
and the newspaper carriers arrive
in their rumbly cars at six a.m.
and throw the papers into the flower beds.

Home is where the family argues
over whether the Thanksgiving turkey was cut
while it was still too hot,
and the children keep their rooms dirty
even when they are grown up.

Home is where you sometimes feel guilty
because not everyone has a home,
so you write a check, and for now home remains
a bright corner of the brain that the atrocities
of life do not penetrate.

Somehow, you are always sane there,
the music of the rain is soft and beautiful,
and it doesn't matter if the stars
run out of fuel someday,
because this is your festival.
The air is cool and sweet,
friends are coming for dinner,
Cassiopeia and Centaurus are in place.

About the Author

Lucille Lang Day's previous poetry collections are *Fire in the Garden* (Mother's Hen) and *Self-Portrait with Hand Microscope* (Berkeley Poets' Workshop and Press), which received the Joseph Henry Jackson Award in Literature. She is a co-author of *How to Encourage Girls in Math and Science: Strategies for Parents and Educators* (Dale Seymour), and the author of the libretto for *Eighteen Months to Earth*, a science fiction opera with music by John Niec. She received her M.A. in creative writing from San Francisco State University, and her M.A. in zoology and Ph.D. in science and mathematics education from the University of California at Berkeley. Currently, she is director of the Hall of Health, a museum in Berkeley, and a lecturer in education at Saint Mary's College of California.